CLXXI

CHASING
CARS

A STORY OF

LOVE, DEATH AND
REDEMPTION

BY SUSAN A. TISO

Forward

This is my story. I am under no illusion that anyone else present for these events would share the same feelings or viewpoints described in this book. My perception, details and descriptions of events are based on my own observations. I do not expect others who were present or otherwise, to agree or dispute my personal stories and account of my life as I have recorded it. This book was written with love and forgiveness, both for me and others so we may all move forward and witness the abundant gifts that being emotionally free can offer. Some names have been changed or omitted out of love and kindness for those individual journeys still in progress in this life.

Namaste' (I bow to the divine in you)

My Emma Rose and Johanna Elena,

It is through your birth that I found real purpose for the first time in my life.

It has been through your support, endless laughter and infinite wit; I have been encouraged to take great risks in every area of my life.

It is the maturity far beyond your years along with the extreme empathy you both possess; that allowed me to take your grandfather in (and the chaos that ensued) and love him freely until his last breathe.

That did not go unnoticed.

I will always be indebted to you for having compassion as big as the universe and love as deep as the ocean.

I love your guts. ♥

Chapter One

He walked in the front door to my house and passed by me as if I wasn't there.

Like a vagrant begging for spare change—I was invisible. I'd pushed the envelope too far this time. I was going to be completely ignored.

I called looking for the child support he owed my mother that week. When she could not get him to return her calls, I was always her *next step*. Logical, though it seemed to her, it was a desperate move to use a child for such adult matters. Light years away from the ABC's of proper divorce protocol, my anger, frustration, and disloyalty would cost me today.

He barely spoke a word to the mother of his 4 children. Coolly brushing past her as the poison of divorce had all but drained the two of them of any human kindness they previously had for each other to create our family of 6. As my little brother emerged with an old pillowcase full of clothes and Legos for the weekend, and with the same disconnect in which he had entered, my dad, also made his exit.

Hearing the car doors slam, my chest felt heavy and sad. I could feel all the blood in my body rise up to my head and my ears started to ring. I knew my mother would feel rejected by me but I wanted to go with them. At 11 years' old I certainly did not understand the consequences of my actions; not the consequences of that day or the ones I would suffer for many years to come. I was trying to be loyal to my mom who would eventually hand me a love letter my dad had written during their marriage while on a trip to Ireland—written to his mistress and not my mom. The letter that made everything come crashing down and the one weekend he finally took me to his new home, I was instructed to present it to her; to him; to them. I was never invited back, for obvious reasons, which may have been my mom's plan all along. I don't know and I'll never ask her. This letter destroyed our family; the neighborhood parties; the love story. It would crash like a burning building and life would change forever for everyone involved. My last name would eventually change (for spite) and I would go from being a little girl who spent hours making mud pies under the large willow tree in the back yard, to the hostess at holidays, caretaker of everyone's feelings, and being my mom's buddy. This was the skill set I was being given for my entire life—like pushing someone out of an airplane equipped with only a windbreaker, and a pinwheel, strapped to a lifeless mannequin instead of an instructor. I was hurled into a premature adulthood with not even a map. I would make many mistakes and guffaw my way through life, trying to find where I fit in, never regaining what I lost. It would be awkward and painful and I was going to make every fumble in broad daylight for the whole world to see and judge.

I ran out the door, down our front walk. My artist dad made the walkway out of cement just a few years earlier, creatively making every square of the ten he poured into their own story with our names or a cartoon, decorating some with seashells pushed into the now hardened path. On the way to the bus every morning I made a ritual of reading each section, stopping at the one he dedicated to me. It was quite simple—my name with a daisy made out of a few broken clam shells. This was one of the rare times I felt special while growing up—the third girl and "mistake"; until my brother, The Prince, came along. I grew up being told the story of my birth.

"What?! Another girl?!?" my dad was to have said.

I was nothing special to anyone but my mom, who lost the baby before me. She always said she waited so long for me. I spent my entire life wishing I was more special to my dad and less special to my mom.

As I ran that day, my extra-long legs hopped over every other square of the personalized path. Heading for my dad's car from our Cape Cod style house on the corner of Whitlock and Tremont, I had no time to be amused by the cartoon characters or look for my name. I ran from the house of secrets and made a b-line for the street. From a young age, I was instructed not to tell anyone what went on inside. The "lack of" or the excess for which there were always extremes. Either there was too much food or not nearly enough, which did lead to some creative meals notwithstanding my brother's *raw onion and green peppers with French dressing salad.* This was eaten out of a large mixing bowl as our sink was always full of dishes and rancid dish water no matter how many times I stood on the step stool and washed.

There were tag sale items my mother bought or stashed away from my father and for years after, only to resell at our own tag sales with the original price tags still on them. There was the stereo console that was as big as a dining room table, delivered in a huge crate that I was to pretend did *not* in fact get delivered at all when questioned by Nosey-Rosie-Testa across the street who was more concerned than she was nosey. My mom overplayed Connie Francis and Freddy Fender from that thing after my dad left. I would sit under the kitchen table and play Barbie humming "*Who's sorry now?*" instead of nursery rhymes. My dad was out of work a lot and my mother's family often helped financially. I was informed years later by my cousin, that we were considered the "white trash" of the family and this is literally the slogan that had crossed my mind for every family party, wedding, and funeral for decades as I knew who said it and who did not argue. Careless words can hurt and reach far beyond the adults they were intended to reach. I can give my relatives a bit of a pass as my mother settled into her role as the victim of the family quite young, a trait that caused me to strive for the opposite.

As children, we played the part of Gavaroche, the little boy in Les Miserables—we looked sad, hungry, and poor but were given the trademark *flared nostril* and evil eye from my mother when we were offered food at a relative's house. "Do not ask to eat and do not say you are hungry" my mother would instruct us before we got out of the car. The hot baloney sandwiches that baked in the sun on the back window of my mother's old Plymouth for the hour long drive to Mt. Vernon, stuffed in the recycled Wonder bread bag was for us to eat as we made the rounds from one house to another each Sunday.

I remember being hungry most of the time—one reason I think I over ate for so many years because I never knew when I'd eat again, this was also something that kept me from attending school on test days. I hated the silent room echoing my hungry stomach. It was as if my whole class knew I had not eaten since the day before, that my bed had no sheets or pillowcases, the rotted and moldy bathroom we had with no hot water for showers or that my mother had not come home for a few days leaving my brother and me to fend for ourselves once again. I swore my rumbling belly was betraying the many secrets of alcoholism, hoarding and neglect in my home with a few thunderous beats. Being young, you learn to adapt easier I think. The Prince and I made tent cities out of the entire living room and watched Saturday Night Live until our eyes bled. We loved the bees and "no Coke, Pepsi" skits with the drug humor going way over our heads at 8 and 10 years' old. I can still recite a Rosanne Rosanna Dana skit about Dr. Joyce Brothers, a sauna and a tiny little sweat ball. We slept on the hardwood living room floor under a canopy of sheets in front of roaring fires. I will always be amazed we hadn't become a statistic for all the fires we built in the fireplace sometimes for fun and sometimes for heat when our furnace broke and the hot water heater gave way leaving us without either or a way to bathe for almost 3 years. Clearly my brother and I are both meant to be here and we are both pretty good at fire making. He tends to overdo it by making 30 foot flames and burning anything he can get his hands on still pretty impressive stuff.

Not much of an athlete, I made it to Tremont Lane, only to see the back of my dad's car halfway down the street. Thinking I could catch up to his 1970s Chevy Vega, I ran after it. I quickly lost my breath with angry, hot tears streaming down my face, and stopped dead in the middle of the street. The warm June air mixed with the speed of my gate caused a breeze and made each tear sting all the way down to my chin. An unfamiliar voice (mine) half yelled and half cracked, standing with fists clenched, I could feel the veins pop out of my neck as I screamed, "Please take me with you!" My pleading sobs went unnoticed. By then, he was too far away. In the distance, I saw the brake lights at the stop sign as the car turned from Tremont and onto Cherry Lane bound for his new home and his new family, with my little brother and not me. He was gone.

It was Father's Day 1978.

This same man, many years later and way past the selfish arrogance of that Father's Day, would allow only ME to bathe his cancer ravaged body. He chose MY home to die, not his new wife, or my brother "The Prince" or either of my sisters for that matter.

Me.

It occurred to me, I had been chasing cars for over 35 years.

Chapter Two

When I was young I remember sitting on the basement steps, peering out through the slats watching my dad, the artist, sitting at his drafting table. His large recycled Chock Full O' Nuts coffee can filled with pencils as sharp as lead swords, the points sticking up and out, waiting to be a part of the next masterpiece. He would draw cartoons, intricate plans for his next experiment, or perfectly letter a drawing. Those "swords" were not there to cause pain or violence. They created cartoons from my dad's imagination. It was a treat to creep down the basement stairs, looking through the back of the wooden steps undetected for hours, watching the master at work.

My father was 5'10" and weighed about 150 lbs. but to me, he was a giant; at least when I was young. He had the most beautiful, blue eyes and always smelled of his cigarettes, Tarytons. His hands were dry and rough from a severe skin condition and felt like sandpaper most every single day. I did not inherit his artistic influence, but instead, his dry hands. As I held onto them in the last days of his life I remember thinking how much I would miss them; peeling and crusty looking—they were still comforting. To me, those hands were the power behind the "super power". When you are 9, your parents are the gods of your world. You see no flaws, you take threats seriously, and you believe every word they say—even if you're not sure where your dad's position as "The Royal breakfast chef for the King and Queen of Bavaria" falls on his curriculum vitae. This was the story I heard every time he made his famous French toast the royal family apparently loved so much. I was always envious of this royal family until we were served their favorite "egg and tuna salad". It was then I realized this family must have been total barbarians! Gross.

My dad didn't cook a lot. Cooking was my mother's job and reason for living. At any time before my parents' divorce, one could find an enormous pot of Italian "gravy" cooking almost non-stop on the stove filled with meatballs, sausage, large pepperoni sticks, and beef ends. This pot of homemade goodness would cook for days on end. Visitors were offered a piece of Italian bread that was torn off by hand, dipped in the gravy, and plopped on a plate. (The longstanding argument of calling it *sauce* or *gravy* is lost on me. We call it gravy and its good!) If you were lucky enough, you would get a meatball on a fork. No plate needed as this "Italian lollipop" was meant to be eaten quickly. Firstly, because it was rare to be offered a *coveted* meatball and not just the soaked bread; secondly, it was good not adding to the already sink full of dirty dishes.

Decades later, my childhood friend Snookie related her memories of my house before my parents' divorce. She said she would dream about the pot of gravy riding on bus 17 to my house with her sleeping bag rolled under her arm and her Donny Osmond lunch box in hand. She'd enter the door of my tiny, cluttered house, my mom holding down the fort in the kitchen, with the telephone glued to her ear, head cocked to one side to form a death grip between her head and shoulder as the telephone wire stretched into practically every room of the house and certainly further than it was initially designed to go. My mom did this so she would have her hands free to stir the big pot, begin frying eggplant or have lightning speed access to the crock pot full of wooden spoons she could grab like a ninja and swat whoever was out of line. The wooden spoon artistry was usually reserved for my brother. Snookie would go up to my mom with her green eyes speaking the international sign for "feed me" (she recalls with salivary memory) as the piece of crusty Italian bread dripped with the bright red gravy was handed down to her.

When asked what she wanted to be when she grew up, for many years Snookie responded with complete confidence as if it was a real career, "I want to be Italian."

The year my parents separated I was in third grade and had my first male teacher. The first half of the school year was blissful ignorance and, although I don't remember many dates, January 18 (of my third grade school year), was the first time I'd ever heard my parents argue and my dad left—never to return. This is definitely the reason I am quick to collect my things in a relationship and leave after a disagreement on any level. We could disagree about where to go for dinner and all the time I am thinking "well, that was a nice run. Bye." It took me writing this book to realize this terrible habit and there will be a collective "Aha" heard around the world by exes everywhere after reading this book.

These were the last few days of the golden years; blissful ignorance of life, the years I brought my bag lunch to school; a cream cheese and jelly sandwich or a baloney sandwich with black cherry soda I would often trade the soda for the goodies the "normal kids" packed. Kids whose parents I assumed came over on the Mayflower and did not arrive through one of our nations ports around the turn of the century like my grandparents; kids who seemed "normal" to me because WASP was normal in my suburban town and having a mother who spoke fluent Italian was different. Only one other kid, Tony (of course) trumped me as his parents came straight from Italy and we talk about how different we were because of that to this day. Twinkies and Doritos were traded with a "no-givesies-backsies" policy that was respected with the bag lunchers. I was soon to be a lunch-ticket-kid unbeknownst to me and even forced to sit at the hot lunch table Monday-Thursday; lest my entire table stared at my tray of Salisbury steak and anemic green beans. The "lunch ticket" was for economically disadvantaged kids for which there were only a handful at the time; a small but obvious indicator that we were poor. This was something my mother had strongly fought to let anyone really know about in our neighborhood but now my entire school knew and with that, they seemed to know every dark secret in my home, or so it felt as if they did. The cool bag-lunchers only got hot lunch on Pizza-Friday and that is where everyone was equal—just on Pizza-Friday.

My third grade teacher was an Italian man, about my dad's age, with a terrible reputation for being quick to anger. I cried all summer after finding out he was my teacher. He was mean and scary. His whole face would turn beat red at the drop of a hat; not like my dad at all. In his classroom, under the radar was the best place to be.

One day he caught me chewing gum.

"Susan McCarthy!"

He called me up to the front of the class—his whole head changing color as I slowly walked to the front of the now silent room towards his outstretched hand—pink then dark pink then into the red family, the shades of his skin became darker and darker at the mere thought of my heinous, albeit, non-violent crime. As I reached the front of the now silent room trembling, I swore I could feel the inferno of Hades coming off of him. Reaching into my mouth, I pulled out my gum. It was then I noticed his soft, mushy almost woman-like hands. In an instant, I was empowered to stand up to this obviously weak, effeminate man who was nothing more than a bully because a REAL man has hands that are MANLY and calloused and peeling from REAL work. A real man pours cement and builds things, although rarely finishes them, but he has tools and stuff, and a drafting table—like my dad! Feeling a burst of courage, I took my gum and slammed it into the palm of his hand, saliva dripping through his fingers and with a smirk I skipped back to my seat as if I had slayed a dragon; head held high and strutting. I never looked at him the same way again.

Decades later, I sat holding my father's still calloused and strong yet tired hands. These were the same hands that helped save a young child and her mother some 40 years earlier at the Beardsley Zoo. The little girl wanted to feed the "cute dogs" but the "dogs" were actually wolves. The wolf cage was a low chain link fence and when the little girl tried to share her sandwich, she became lunch! By the time my father and another man hopped the fence to help, one of the wolves had gotten ahold of the mothers arm as well. As the wolves tried to rip the two through the fence, my father grabbed rocks, and made fists to punch them. The other man got pretty torn up but my dad's hands were not exactly a delight for the wolves and they were mysteriously ignored him. Before help arrived, my dad was able to get several good shots in (he was positioned the closest to them) without being attacked. As the ambulance carted away the mother, daughter, and the other blood soaked man, my father casually walked back to his family of 6 and we left as if it were just another day at the zoo.

Now these "hero-hands" were attached to a body that contained only a few organs working at about 20% capacity. For weeks I desperately tried to lotion—these hands—hoping if I could mend one crack I could quite possibly stop the cancer that was in his brain, lungs, liver, stomach, and shrink the large tumor that wrapped around his back. Maybe I could lotion him into remission? There were times he would look at me before the

Morphine slowly kidnapped his spirit, and would flash his signature smirk. When I was young, that smirk used to come across as condescending; leaving any one of the McCarthy children feeling toyed with or accepted like his buddy, depending on which child you were. This "smirk" replaced our difficult conversations; our discussions about the past and what I perceived as our apologies to each other. Yes—a little smirk was all of that. Back in those last days, when he flashed "the smirk" I felt helpless and pathetic. Maybe I was too fragile to actually talk it out; perhaps there was really nothing left to say. Certainly nothing said could change the past or magically change my future.

Chapter Three

The day my dad came home to my
house to die was warm and sunny. I
am grateful this one and only time for
global warming and the 3 glorious
weeks I had left with him that Indian
summer of 2009. I stood outside of
Burlington Coat Factory 1 hour before
they opened, knocking firmly but
respectfully on the glass door. A sales
associate came to the door irked and
ready to educate me on just what
"10:00-open" means at 9:00 am.
Before she could start I hysterically
but diligently word vomited the
following, "I'm springing my dad
from the hospital in 30 minutes, he's
only got weeks to live, and my sister
is singing the national anthem at The
Taste of Danbury. I need him to look
his very best; he's very important to

me". She was obviously moved. Teary eyed, she let me in. "I lost my dad too" she said and we are instantly part of "the club". The club you don't think is a big deal until you are granted membership. The club where it's the first time you must admit, you are going to be an orphan at age 43 and, as silly as it sounds, you are reduced to childish emotions. All the maturity you thought you had in order to deal with life as an adult comes into question. She did not allow other associates to get within 10 feet of me and there were lots of dirty looks as they sleepily set up for the day. I purchased Ralph Lauren colored boxers, Roca Wear socks, a Ralph Lauren pull-over, blue shirt, Puma sweats, and the coolest jean jacket I could find. I paid, grateful, and in a panic that he wouldn't be there when I got back; I headed up the street to the 11th floor of the hospital.

He was resting when I got to the hospital and true to his personality he popped up and said "Let's go!" I dressed him and we exited. Tears streamed down my face, behind my sunglasses as I guided his borrowed wheelchair across the city green. I finally had my dad where I wanted him. Hell, I HAD a dad! Ready to show him off to everyone I knew and the impact of how I was able to lasso him into this excursion had not even fully hit me. He would *have* to be dying to commit to anything regarding his kids let alone allow me to be in charge. He did however "direct" his explorations around the festival by barking directions and pointing left or right where he wanted to go. At one point I had enough and said "Watch it old man you can't make it to the car alone!" 20 years ago I would've gotten a tap on the belt—instead he just smirked and laughed with me. God I liked this guy. Where was my scary, unapproachable dad? Can I keep "dying-dad" but like, he doesn't actually die?

Chapter Four

There was a bit of a tussle for my dad in the hospital as my sister wanted him with her. They were close, very close. They had a special bond and my sister has a way of acting as if she was his only child and we were all illegitimate. I keep asking my mom but she sticks to her story that we were all the product of their marriage. I remember the look on her face when he gently (again not the guy I grew up with) told her he was going home to my house to get well. She was so hurt and I felt her pain. I didn't revel in being chosen. I never felt like I was more important than her I just felt he was probably being smart. My sister appeared to be in charge as she threw me out of my own kitchen and did the intake with hospice. To this day I have no idea what the proper protocol was supposed to be or the signs of the end as she chose to keep it all to herself. I think she was hoping he would eventually come back to her house. I did what I was told and didn't ask questions. Something magical happens when I'm in the presence of my siblings. I'm reduced to a skinny, 9 year old, blonde waif. When my older sisters get together they can be quite a force. I try to stand up to them but the age difference keeps us a bit disconnected, among other reasons. They both left right after my dad and my brother and I marvel how we grew up born of the same two people, but in completely different families from our sisters.

My screened in porch would prove to be the backdrop for most of the visitors, conversations, and the tall tales my dad would spin in those last days. He would start with his ritual morning cigarette—even when the drugs started to consume his thoughts—his Tarryton was invisible to the naked eye. It was a habit ingrained in him since his childhood growing up the son of Irish immigrants in New York's Hell's Kitchen. I toyed with him one day as he held his empty fingers in the position, extending his arm as dramatically as he could so they were far from me.

"What are you doing daddy?"

"I'm just trying to keep my cigarette from getting smoke in your face". He was so thoughtful, especially because there was no cigarette in his hand.

I chuckled with delight at this playful dad of mine. He was so docile on pain killers; far from the memory of the man who once had me and my brother leap to attention like a Von Trapp child as they heard their fathers whistle; only there was no whistle, just the tap on his belt buckle like the warning shot before a whipping. We were terrified of getting the belt, yet to this day I don't remember getting hit with it even once. My dad was not loud, but he did command respect. We had a healthy fear of our parents, a character trait that seems all but lost on children today.

The day he came home from the hospital was very busy. In the late afternoon, everyone went back to their homes and it was just me and my dad. Tears welled up in my eyes and I bit my lip to try and keep them from tumbling down my cheeks.

I said to him, "I just got you back, you can't leave me now". My dad was not fond of hysterics or tears. He was, however, a softy on the inside. He looked at me with the smirk he was famous for and said "oh it's gonna be fine" as if I had fallen and skinned my knee. He came from a very stoic, Irish mother. There was no affectionate hug with that sentence; just the smirk, and his dancing blue eyes trying to dismiss my anxiety. We never discussed our past relationship again. That day I let him off Scott free for his bad behavior... and he let me off just the same for mine.

The first few days of his stay, he would get up off of my couch unassisted and talk about how he was only sleeping over for a short time before going back home. He had spent the last two years since moving back from England, building a salvage vessel in the carport of a friend's home. He made the one-man boat from scratch and had mapped out his course. He studied the plight of a ferry that had burned for many miles until it sank. He believed the crew threw items off the boat from the start before it came to rest and no one had really searched the fiery path before it rested in its watery grave. They only looked at the wreckage sight for artifacts. He was due to connect the computer in a few weeks and launch it into the Long Island Sound to look for his buried treasure.

The boat was destroyed after he died and that was tough on the grandkids who watched him build it, my sisters youngest, Zachary, was his apprentice. I think he took it the hardest; such a special time in a young man's life to learn next to the Master and be related to the legend. He was certainly a fascinating, creative person. I don't think my father noticed his own age except when he saw his reflection in the mirror each morning. He was ageless when it came to hopes and dreams. Only death could keep my dad from this adventure or did it in fact, allow for more adventure?

In the mornings I would "spot" him to the bathroom where I honored his dignity and pride and closed the door. Standing on the other side, I would press my ear against the door as hard as I could to make sure he wasn't crashing into the walls. After he was done I would assist him to the porch where he would sit in my rocking chair with a cup of coffee and his cigarettes. It was during these times I would scurry into the living room and change the sheet and pillowcases he slept on as he was starting to sweat a lot from the opiates. I refused to allow him to smell ill or look unkempt.

Every day I would coax him into eating a bite of something to stay nourished. He ate a bit here and there as not to hurt my feelings. I can see how easy it must be for an addict to lose track of personal hygiene and even food with such powerful drugs. My dad was a lightweight; 150 lbs. soaking wet. A Bud Light was as hard as he ever went.

One morning, thinking he was sound asleep, I crept towards the front door, late for my brand new job as an elementary school secretary. He popped his head up over the back of the couch as I tried not to wake him while I grabbed my purse.

"Did the doctor say I have 6 to 8 months or 6 to 8 weeks?" he asked matter-of-factly.

I went pale. When this was discussed in the hospital, I was surrounded by my siblings and 2 highly regarded doctors from the prestigious Praxair Center in Danbury, and whereas relations were strained with my dysfunctional family, we were all together getting this news, there was a sense of support and camaraderie.

Now, I stood there alone, frozen and late for work, choking back the tears as I replied almost inaudibly "6 to 8 weeks, daddy". He seemed to ponder the answer for a moment as if I just let him know we were out of the good coffee and I needed to mix him up a Nescafe' with toilet water.

"Okay," he replied as I went to work for one of the last times until after his death.

Chapter Five

Most days, everyone would come, eat, visit, and leave. One day, after I ran around waiting on people and feeding everyone in my small 1960s kitchen that did NOT have a dishwasher, my older sister (bending down) said,

"We're leaving now. By the way, daddy seems to have messed himself. Bye".

"Really??" I thought to myself.

In the end, I had spent most every waking hour caring for him. I ended up interfacing with the nurses, doctors, and hospice. I was an authority on medication's purpose and amounts. The Florence Nightingale part of me took to that easily. My OCD side, kept charts and graphs documenting all of it. I required people to initial medication administrations and flipped like a new mother when I found he was not given his meds one night because "he seemed fine"—Shirley MacLaine in "Terms of Endearment" came to mind over and over. I couldn't stop him from dying but I sure as hell wasn't going to let him be in pain. That, of course, was within the first week, when I thought I could still lead two lives.

I had taken a "safe", low paying job in a bad economy after my unemployment ran out and I was now an elementary school secretary. The parents and kids aside, I was despised from day 2 by my principal and it ended up being a horrible experience. The frigid woman was quite vocal about her hatred for her own parents and she did not appreciate her school being left to a (perfectly qualified) sub for 2 weeks while I endured this journey instead of leaving my dad on the cancer floor of the hospital to die. In those first couple of days, one highly regarded teacher quietly took me aside and told me to do what I needed to do because there are "no do-overs in death". She was the least likely person to stick her neck out and for that, I was grateful for the "family" of educators that enveloped me almost immediately when I needed it the most. Over the years I heard the principal had lost her parents and I always wonder if she ever learned the lesson of empathy.

Emma, my oldest, had just started college and stayed hidden as much as possible from all of this. She's sweet, sensitive, and I do suppose that was how she dealt with it. I will also add to my list of mommy-demerits, the fact that I did not notice nor did I ask her how she was feeling. In my defense, I was a little busy, but Emma was my personal rock through my own health challenges, wise beyond her years. She was bestowed an unfair responsibility and never complained. My youngest was just starting 7th grade and there were days I just kept her home to spend time with her grandfather and family. My call to the absentee-hotline would say,

"Jo can't make it to school today, she is spending time with her grandfather as he is leaving this earth soon and that is not a life lesson you can teach. Thank you."

Watching the drugs take over and escalate his demise was tough to see. My dad was a gleeful drunk and his slight build did not allow for heavy partying of any sort, after a few Budweiser's he was done. He never took drugs, recreationally or otherwise. This medication regimen was tough for him to deal with. I came home to find "The Artist" sketch one of his famous cartoon characters of himself. It was a man with an IV pole. He wrote "OxyContin 20 mg…100 mg". This was his way of expressing how fast they had increased the dosage in just 5 days. The next day he had a hallucination that led him outside holding a sign he made on an envelope. He said he was trying to warn my brother to be careful, the police were looking for him. Apparently in his day dream my brother had made some idle threats and was on the lam. I was at work when I got the call from my dad that The Prince was in trouble (dad said he would be sitting on the front steps waiting to warn him), I dropped everything and headed home. Twelve minutes later—there was my dad just as he said—sitting on my front step. The sign he held perfectly straight so no one would miss it. Of course, I called my brother on my way home screaming at him; I was shocked when he told me he had been at work all day. I took my dad in the house and sat him down. There was no argument, there was no police presence canvasing the neighborhood. My brother who was the closest to my dad but had a falling out those last few years had come to see him in the hospital but that was it. My dad would "speak" to my brother often or so he thought. I would look around for who he was intently having a conversation with and all I saw was thin air. He would call me *Joey* and seemed disappointed when I would say,

"No daddy, it's me, Susie".

Joey had not been to my house that week. To the end I know my dad thought that whole thing was real. It took him hours of asking me to reassure him it never happened for him to settle down. Sixteen days later he was gone.

Chapter Six

Facebook entry: September 24, 2009

*He paints a mural in the air w/
imaginary brushes, I hold his hand &
my fingers become his finest pens, he
exchanges pleasantries with
passengers on a bus I cannot see, he
is waiting on a dock for a ferry "see
that woman?" he points to the
fireplace "she takes the tickets", his
blue eyes look directly into mine, he
says "I'm not here anymore" & I am
left standing on the dock watching the
ferry slowly break thru the waves.*

As a young child, before I became the
enforcer for the child-support-mafia-
collection-agency, I had the reputation
of being the "Florence Nightingale"
of my family. I was tall and lanky and

at that time; quiet. I would play for hours under the willow tree in the back yard making mud pies in a broken Susie Homemaker oven that was a hand-me-down from a cousin. I was always ready to entertain my older sisters with a Shirley Temple song or make funny faces to get people to laugh. I was a nurturer and a pleaser from day one. Whether I was aware of people's moods and sadness by doing my song and dance to cheer them up or tuning into who had cramps and filling the hot water bottle, I was, and have always been driven to be a 'first responder'. It's a wonder I didn't go into nursing but I really can't stand the thought of a needle puncturing skin. I was always the sickly one and yet I was there with the napkins, wadded up, and dripping with cold water for whoever had a fever or bunched up toilet paper with scotch tape to dress a wound or scrape. Once, when my sister fell and skinned her knee wide open, I ran to the bathroom and grabbed the biggest band aid I could find. I ran through the yard towards her and the group of older neighborhood teens who had collected around her. I shouted triumphantly, "its okay. I got it! I'll help you Sissy!" clutching a large Kotex in my spindly hand waving it back and forth; I would fix her.

I was hard-wired to think I could save the world by turning bloody scratches into healing scabs, then later, try to turn unimaginative lovers who lacked ambition for more than the remote control, into someone worthy of my time. I now found myself completely devastated because I knew for sure I had no power for salvation at all. My father was dying. I was racing with the clock and I wasn't sure how to tie up the loose ends. There were times in my life I felt helpless but this was a shattering blow to the "me" I thought I was all my life. Past lovers had been allowed to syphon every ounce of life sustaining energy from me in order for them to feel good or the ones who would exploit my innocent need for love, paled in comparison to this life event. This was going to be my biggest failure yet.

No lotion, no humor, no wadded up toilet paper, or really big band aid was going to stop the inevitable and I could do nothing but watch.

Chapter Seven

Facebook entry: September 29, 2009

Reminiscent of being a new mother, I sleep when he sleeps so I can be alert when he's awake, I am walking around in sweats, ponytail, and I'm not gonna lie, I haven't shaved my legs in weeks. I can't remember my life before this and I can't imagine my life when this is over...

My brother-in-law made a comment after observing me during these precious last 21 days of my dad's life. He said, "You have the heart of a servant". I remember feeling instantly offended. I was so tired but always tried to make sure everyone was fed and comfortable. Now I just felt like a maid. Seeing the look on my face he said, "Sister-in-law" (He calls me

Sue-Babe or Sister-in-law and I find it endearing) "Sister-in-law', he said, 'the heart of a servant has honor in God's eyes". Heaven knows I could've used all the honor and favor from God I could get my hands on, but I was never doing it for that. I did it for my dad, my family, and in hopes that my heart would somehow be mended or at least not be as fragile as it seemed to be for the last 40 years. I had never been truly loved and I was convinced it was because I was unlovable.

There were visitors every day and I'd set up my kitchen to host the constant parade that filtered through my tiny ranch house. It was your standard hotel style breakfast bar with a toaster, coffee pot, and an assortment of muffins, bagels, jams, jellies, waffles, English muffins, and cereal.

At about 11:00 am it would get broken down and put away and the chafing dishes would come out in order to display the trays of lasagna, eggplant parm, salads, and breads to feed the masses. I had been up making food from 1:00 am – 4:00 am every night the week he was in the hospital. People were kind and changed it up for my guests and family by bringing soups and other meals I wasn't proficient in cooking (to this day my kids have banned me from making lasagna—they are so sick of it). Again. I thought, if food could save him, I would live in my kitchen the rest of my life. I wasn't used to caretaking for people who died. Everyone got better, always. It's a terrible day when you realize just how powerless you are and for a bossy, control freak like me, this was brutal.

My porch was set up with various games from Milton Bradley personifying my childhood as well as that of my siblings. "Don't Break the Ice" became a favorite for the 13 – 26 yr. old nieces and nephews. Yes, for those of you who know the game it IS incredibly annoying for adults— especially when the ice cubes fall and the man on the chair in the center, would crash against my antique 1940s metal farm table—worse when it is played by teenage kids. My dad loved the chaos and movement of the grandkids, their friends, relatives, and clatter of dishes. I liken it to Easter Sunday, but for 21 days and in the end there was only death with absolutely no resurrection.

Chapter Eight

My parents together produced 4 children and we all collectively produced 11 grandchildren for them. Did I mention that they brought their friends to my hospitality hospice? Yes, my house was more of a family gathering on a holiday, than a sad hospice. For the man who could not spend more than an hour or two in the same room with his kids for decades, we were everywhere, we weren't leaving and he could not escape. A few years earlier, my sister had invited us all to visit with my dad at the local Sycamore diner. It's a cute little landmark in our town where they still offer car hop service and have the best steak sandwich. We all sat down, ordered our food, and before it was served, he stood up, announced he was leaving and it was nice to see us and walked out—my sister's mouths hanging open—these were the scraps I had been used to for years.

Unlike that day, my dad was now a captive audience and on several occasions he was forced into a conversation to have that defining moment of reconciliation with everyone except me.

On the rarest of occasions a few months earlier when my oldest daughter, Emma, graduated high school, I threw a huge house party. It was mostly for family as we are a traveling party in size and exuberance. The party was complete with my friend's rock band playing on the sun deck. The police were summoned at 11:05 pm (by a neighbor) and after I failed to bribe the nice officer with a piece of lasagna to go and a cup of coffee, the party continued anyway, sans the rock band, until 3:00 am. Oddly, Dad would not leave. He sat in the corner of the porch in a blue velvet, wingback chair I had dragged outside from my living room earlier in the day for my mom. He looked like Dick Cavett ready to interview Jacques Cousteau. I believe he knew then his time was short and this is why he stayed watching the kids and adults dance on the porch into the wee hours of the morning. He called several times that week to tell me that was "one hell of a party Susz". It was unlike my dad to reach out just to compliment me. I suspect when a person feels their life is shortly coming to a close, it must be hard to grasp it all. Trying to make up for all the lost time one shamefully wastes must seem impossible and sad. I don't think it's as easy as the movies make it out to be where you realize time is short and you make a pilgrimage to tell everyone you love them or have an awkward and contrived game of catch with your grown son for some sort of instant healing. We are so complex in our will and just as stubborn that I would think pride must make it a virtual nightmare to be face to face with your regrets. For me, now at the half century mark, I already have a mental list of things I wish I did better, words I never spoke and words I wish I had. I changed my last name at the age of 18 to bring even more distance to our virtually non-existent relationship and with the secret hope of never feeling the pain of rejection again—it didn't work, of course, and I now know it caused him great pain adding to the already huge gap in the much needed connection between a father and daughter. A very childlike move made out of hurt and anger for someone just entering adulthood—this would prove to be my M.O. in all relationships for many decades. Trying to erase each man who came into my life and left as if they never existed; giving back gifts, deleting photos, even if it was amicable. It's a wonder I didn't end up making my living dancing on a pole with all these "daddy issues" I have. Certainly, one doesn't need a pole or obvious destructive lifestyle choice to show they are broken on the inside. My pathology has been the thing that has drawn many men to me, that mix of vulnerability and strength. It was always my desire to break free from being a victim that drove the bad ones away, those men who liked the bird with the broken wing and wanted to fix it but keep it in a cage forever and never let it fly. If I was doing well and feeling strong, I wasn't allowed to show weakness with men who expected my sharp, tough side. Apparently, I can't be both. A constant battle rages inside of me, vying for the attention and security that my father; with the calloused, peeling hands was supposed to give and trying to not be affected by the rejection I felt every day for decades. It may have seemed a futile attempt for my dad to try to make up being an absentee parent. To admit leaving his 4 young children only to take up with a woman who had 5 train wreck teenagers of her own could not be easy. How could he make any of this up to us?

…Or to me?

Facebook Entry: September 28, 2009

It was a shipwreck that kept us up last night it must have been horrible because dad was quite upset he tried to help the passengers many times to no avail. As he quieted down I held his hand & he whispered "I love you". (I froze) knowing it wasn't for me I asked who he was talking to "My mother" he said & I know THEY are making the journey to come get him & bring him to his new home where there is no pain & no more suffering.

Chapter Nine

1 year earlier… the standard grade, florescent overhead lights moved like a sterile light show over my head. I could hear talking but the OR staff must have already started to sedate me for surgery as we were careening down the hallway—gurney, hospital staff, and my dad—I couldn't focus on their faces but it was clear that my fiancé, who tried to enter my hospital room not 4 minutes earlier, was not there. He and my dad were just making their way into my room following behind my stretcher from CT scan as my tiny Asian surgeon blew past them, reprimanding them to stay outside until we spoke. It was a blur of medical jargon but I understood the words, "sepsis" and "less than an hour to live". The

confident and usually in-control doctor had a faint twinge of perspiration that was starting to form across her forehead.

I was to be married for the first time, 5 months from now to a sweet, but overgrown man-child who was a mama's boy begging to be set free. If he had gotten the chance to spend the rest of his life figuring out how to actually make a washing machine work or push a shopping cart through a grocery store with his own list, I honestly think he would've been glad to break his mother's heart. I took great pleasure in daydreaming about his mother, watching her sob while eating her Special K, a milk container sitting beside her bowl that showed his 50 year old, unshaven likeness in his Ranger jersey with the word, "MISSING".

We were closing on our house that week and he was already irritated that I just had surgery 2 days earlier. I will admit I babied him in the same way she did, keeping things from him so he wouldn't be stressed. I had committed to being the sole bread winner so he could play cool step-dad to my girls. It made him happy to walk the hallways of his old middle and high school. Show up for track meets and bring their forgotten lunch. He was good to them but we were about to see what he was made out of when it came to me.

I must have looked dumbstruck because there was silence and then another plea for my permission to operate immediately.

"Do I have your permission to operate?!?!" my once cool doctor now demanded.

"Duh... I mean, yes, of course. I trust you" I said trying to cover my fear with lame humor.

Looking up, Rick was not holding my hand, but my dad was, telling me it would be ok. The first time he has comforted me or been with me for a medical need since I was about 5. Back then, he would hold me down to put drops in my forever infected ears or administer—what seemed like my permanent diet of penicillin as I screamed and thrashed—the only attention reserved exclusively for me growing up. Here he was after all those lost years and I thought, "Really? So this is how it ends?"

Chapter Ten

I woke up from surgery with my flawlessly beautiful surgeon sitting on the side of my bed.

"Did you eat peas???"

I had to think for a minute. I was foggy from the anesthesia and I also have a sense of humor AND a tiny case of a defensiveness.

Peas.

Hmmmm. Is this a trick question or am I in trouble? I mean, really??? IS THIS A TRICK QUESTION OR AM I IN TROUBLE?

I suddenly remembered I HAD eaten mashed peas when I was discharged from the hospital just a few days ago. After what she told me post-op that day, I wasn't sure if I could ever eat anything that wasn't pureed again. What a hell of a shit-show she had to clean-up. My botched gastric by-pass from 4 years before left me reeling over the blatant negligence that took place and my former doctors complete arrogance to leave me so damaged and not tell me anything more than, "Boy did you take up my entire day. YOU were a real problem."

"Yes, I ate peas." I said, like a child in trouble.

"I know. They were EVERYWHERE!" she giggled.

The intestinal surgery (a few days before) to try and put my organs back where God had intended them was actually a huge success. My lungs were collapsed after she pulled the gastric pouch out of my esophagus but I was expected to have a full recovery. I guess my intestines having been shoved under my rib cage for 4 years made them limp and pliable and well, I burst at the seams.

My wonderful doctor again promised a full recovery and accounted for every "pea" that she saw floating around.

My dad was there to hold my hand. He didn't say much, but it felt good to not have to be so strong on my own for once. I had so wished my fiancé was the one there instead since we were closing on our forever home that week. I quickly shrugged that negative feeling aside when I decided I was just being selfish and ungrateful for what I did have. My life was coming together and this was just a bump in the road (I told myself). Everything was going to be fine and look I even had my dad back in my life. The story should've just ended right there ...and they lived happily ever after. The end.

Three weeks later, one hospital-hosted house closing, and several days of my family's help, sans my fiancé, to move my condo belongings into our new home I did not get my happily ever after. I literally lost as close to everything I worked for in the blink of an eye.

My employer, to whom I had delivered his goal of becoming a $1million dollar medical office a year earlier than expected, decided he could hand things over to his wife to run. Of course I left an organized and detailed 5-year-plan for his practice in the bottom right hand drawer of my file cabinet in the office, so there would be little struggle for them if they just continued to follow my plan.

Job gone—check!

I had already realized that my future health would be compromised moving on. I could try to paste on that smile and put that super-hero cape on but the fact is, my tenacious personality would be helpful, if not fool proof. I could not will myself to be well no matter how hard I tried. I could heal quicker and where ever a positive personality would be helpful, it came in handy but it can't make something work that is truly broken. There were things going on inside me undetectable to the naked eye. I went on to have over 100 visits to the hospital and 9 more surgeries. There were no guarantees.

Good health gone—check!

My fiancé, who avoided me as much as possible those first few weeks, could not keep avoiding me once I was mobile again. He was truly remorseful when he said it but it still didn't take away the pain and incredible rejection. He said, he could not "be with someone who was going to be sick all the time". The words hung in the air as he said them. The first time he said them; then the second time he said them; then when he said them to the pastor that was to marry us. When he said them the next dozen or so times after that. I wasn't good enough; hadn't behaved enough or didn't meet yet another man's standards of being agreeable enough to spend time with. He broke our marriage vows before taking them. I was disposable, again. The rejection felt like a quick thrust from a very large, very wide machete. It took my breath away. This is my usual reaction to rejection, no other offense, just rejection. He drove out of my/our driveway, having never moved a pair of pants, a shirt, or a toothbrush IN. He drove down the street and left. The words still hanging in the air and the pain of not being worthy or worth the fight came back like a flood. Holding up a somewhat decent face for my girls, I set out to find a man who would want to be married to someone who might be sick all the time...

or perhaps just to me.

Chapter Eleven

I worked hard to keep my dad comfortable during those last 21 days. There was to be no drama or controversy except my family is full of drama and controversy. The worst part, I was the hostile center of the worst drama there is. Making the Jerry Springer show look more like a memoir than a voyeuristic journey into white trash nation. I called a cease-fire with my sister over a disagreement we had about something she took from me. Granted, I didn't want it anymore, but she started to use it before I was done and some things are just not up for recycling. Some thing's need to be disposed of properly, so the only memories that would eventually re-surface after some fall out, could just be the good ones.

I was standing by the elevators after my dad was moved from the ER to the cancer floor—phone in hand, of course, I was the one to make the call.

"What?" is how my sister answered her phone when I called, making it so much worse than if she didn't already know who was calling her.

"I… a... daddy's in the hospital." I stammered. We had not spoken in 4 years since my children came home from a weekend at their fathers and asked, "Why does daddy blow kisses to Aunt Rosalee?" My wildest and darkest thoughts were true but the fact is, I left him and there was nothing I could do about it, especially since they denied it over and over. My entire family, aunts, uncles, cousins all sided with her lame story of friendship with my children's father because apparently it's better to believe one family member suffers from paranoid ideation than to think of the alternative. There were some who were just mean about it—like being back in middle school and being the least popular person on the playground—that kind of mean. I have never recovered. No one in my family has ever apologized for believing her lie over the truth and ostracizing me publically and passively for years.

After a contentious battle for child support and visitation that I liken to the news clips you see at Christmas when people fight over the most popular toy, and 4 years after the affair "officially" started, my ex had finally admitted his wrong doing and in a tearful series of phone calls that lasted over a week, he asked me to forgive him for that and all the affairs he had while we were together.

In the end, that's all I ever wanted—an apology. I mean, you can't un-ring that bell but acknowledging the destruction it caused was a good way to help me move on. Of course she had dumped him for some slick talking poser but suffered greatly for that in the end. Nothing I wish on anyone, not even my sister. A favorite author of mine describes forgiveness as carrying around a bag of wet socks. That's why I forgive, that and the threat of looking aged and wrinkled.

"Yeah? So what's the matter with him?" my sister asked with complete contempt for me. Something I will never understand to this day since I was not the offender.

"It's cancer, and it's everywhere." I spoke somewhat timidly due to the fractured relationship but also because I was tired and still in shock and frankly, this would've been the sister I wanted to lean on. Rosalee was my oldest sister and I worshiped her when I was growing up. She loved disco and wore super cool clothes. She taught me how to dance and every Saturday she pushed all the living room furniture against the wall while we watched American Bandstand. Soul Train came on after but I was usually ready to play Barbies by then. I was 7 ½ years younger than her. My sisters were teens when my dad left, albeit hurting in their own way, but old enough to speak their mind and by-pass getting caught in the middle of the divorce, like my brother and I did. My dad saw my sisters quite often since the divorce or at least more often than me and without the same hostility.

This reconciliation of sorts would prove to be complicated for many years. I will always love the person she is inside, the person I knew when we were young, I love her need to take any small child she knows and strip their feet of socks and shoes so they can feel the grass or sandy beach on their tiny toes, but I've been kicked in the head and realize, you can never go back and seamlessly find your way to that original place of love and trust again. I can love, but I dare not trust my feelings, my secrets or my life events with someone who has sold me out more than a few times and when I needed her compassion the most. This is not for me to live with, it's for her. I can only give all

my fears and blessings to the universe
for her restoration and mine.

Chapter Twelve

In the short few days my dad was in my home and realized he wasn't going to leave, he summoned my mother. These two people had not spoken to one another, at least civilly in over 30 years. My mother would call me pleading to see him the week he was in the hospital. I stopped answering my phone. The anger I had for all the wasted years, I was clearly holding against her, was choking me now that he was leaving for good.

Nope. You will not cause grief and havoc when I'm trying to cure this cancer with love.

Love and lasagna.

No way lady.

The day my mother arrived, my adult siblings and I became as infantile and goofy as Patty Dukes character in The Parent Trap. We were giddy and almost embarrassed in a goose bumpy-watching-a-kiss-when-you-are-eleven-kind-of-way.

"I'd like to speak to your mother… alone." My father told us and she walked into my living room to where my dad was holding court that evening.

After about 30 minutes and with bated breath, I glanced into the living room to find my dad trying to "open" my 'pull out couch' so he could make room for my mom to sleep next to him.

"Dad! First of all, it's not a pullout couch. Second of all—ew!"

The details of what was said can be speculated upon but the fact is he spent the entire night holding her hand until they drifted off to sleep, he lying on the couch, her sitting in a chair next to him. Much to the chagrin of my father's bossy and crusty Irish sister who descended on my doorstep from Albany demanding "I'm here to see my brother!" my mom was a fixture almost every day until he died. He would ask where she was and wanted her to be comfortable. My aunt didn't like my mom but she also didn't care for my sister so I let her stay until he died. I needed some support and she was a fan of mine the day she arrived.

Meanwhile, my children's father, whom I had done some driving for on movie sets to earn cash after losing my job and his losing my sister, was nowhere to be found.

Delivering 32 cars to be driven by 32 mostly inexperienced drivers (inexperienced working on films) to a major Leonardo Dicaprio/Kate Winslet movie, made me realize what a great working team my ex and I were if not as life partners. He brought the cars and drivers and I organized them. Matching up car makes, models, color, and driver with the walkie-talkie the director assigned them proved helpful to the production assistant and made me feel I had a worthy place in this man's life after all. Maybe I did matter to someone. I always needed to be important to a man, but I needed to be loved and/or needed for me. As I sat in a vintage Ford Thunderbird on a 2 mile stretch of CT highway, in the pitch black, waiting for that first call over the walkie-talkie from the director with my next move, I would get "the visits". My ex would come up, under the guise of checking the car battery in my trunk which powered the aviator landing lights that replaced the regular headlights in each antique car for effect in this scene. The batteries would die out after a few hours and his assistant would skate down the dark highway on his roller blades, replacing batteries, and checking on drivers throughout the evening and into the long overnight before we got the call about an hour before sun up to start the scene. It's a pivotal time in the movie where the lead actors are in a fight on the side of the road. If you watch it, you will be shocked to know we all went to wardrobe for that scene. Not only are we not distinctive, but I'm pretty sure we could have been driving Ford Focuses instead of antique cars. All you see are those bright headlights. I sat listening to my ex lament his break-up (with my sister) and assured him, he would be ok. It was a lot to swallow when I had made a baby with this man and he never cried over me. We were friends, if anything—he was my replacement father figure all those years. At the point when he confessed, and I accepted his apology, I felt a bit more secure that I was looked after once again. Although it was only for a season, and like my father, his love was conditional.

Devastated by the news of my father's ultimate demise, I reached out to my ex. His irrational response for allowing my sister and her new jerk to come and visit was more than I could comprehend. I never reveled in his loss, although a lesser person would have done cartwheels. He knew from the years we were together, the pain of trying to get my dad to visit or acknowledge me was hurtful and he could only think of "loyalty".

Loyalty???

Loyalty???

I not only started working side by side with him but I invited him and his new/old girlfriend to every single holiday and event in our daughter's lives just to show MY loyalty.

I played nice in the sandbox.

"Please just come early to drop Jo off today, so you don't run into them" I begged that Sunday afternoon.

"That's my children's house!! You can't let her in!" he was mean and intimidating and that's just one of the reasons I left him 7 years earlier without taking a fork, knife, or spoon. I was not going to fight over stuff like my parents did. My hope was that would've made it easier for us to get along and not affect the children as much. Out of the 56 cars he owned, I didn't even get the 1992 Buick Roadmaster station wagon I had been driving while every other mom in the affluent community we lived in drove mini vans. He gave it to my sister to drive just to add insult to injury. I fought hard not to fight and in the end, if I didn't comply, I was cut out. Unlike the mob, I wasn't put out of my misery and left at the bottom of the Hudson River with cement shoes to die. Instead, my texts were not acknowledged and my calls were ignored to the point where I just didn't exist, the perfect way to crush me, which he knew.

"I'm not coming in. This is a huge disrespect", he said as I tried to coax him in. He tossed the load of overnight bags; oversized stuffed animals they fought about taking back and forth each week and backpacks the girls had packed from the trunk of his 1964 Mercury that was parked grandly in my driveway.

Too exhausted to fight, I just carried everything inside, not realizing how this one day would change so much in the coming years for me and the girls. This rejection and alienation would be obvious in future gatherings, graduations, and I'll assume, unless the universe is kind, future weddings and grandbabies.

He fired up the old metal beauty as well as a Lucky Strike, adjusted his hat, and drove off; once again someone taking a piece of my heart when I needed it the most and like I had learned a long time ago, running after that car won't change a thing. It won't change someone's heart. It was supposed to toughen mine but I think it only made it more vulnerable.

I walked back into the house to begin a journey alone again of which I would not fully comprehend its lessons for several years.

Chapter Thirteen

That summer, I stood on the stage at the famous Caroline's on Broadway. I had walked up the steps, mouth so dry my lips were stuck to my teeth, my mind completely blank. *(Come on Susan! You know this front and back!)* Looking out to the great NY crowd, and over to my friends who had come and then my oldest daughter; I felt proud. Proud that I did something people only dream of, proud to show my bright and sassy first born she could make all her dreams come true and proud for not falling up the stairs. My opening line was shaky.

"How ya'll doonen?"

(Ya'll??? Doonen?? "What is "Doonen?"")

(Panic). Just breathe. Talk. Just start talking!!

I licked my lips and unstuck them from my teeth. I got out my first joke and the horror on the faces in the front row, softened. I got my first laugh and for the next 10 minutes I owned the world. I paced that stage like a crack whore looking for a john! I was on fire!!

Then I was done.

The whole summer went like that, well mostly like that. I bombed really bad once and almost got into a fight with some angry, tattooed heckler who worked at Borders but decided to get in my car and leave lest I get ambushed by her counterparts.

It was the weekend before Labor Day and I was offered a paying gig every Saturday night at a popular New

Haven comedy club. Things were looking up for me on so many fronts except of course, with men. My last relationship that summer ended it almost before it could begin.

At the end of the end of the brief, almost two week affair, he decided I wasn't "political wife material" with a laundry list of reasons. So there I was, not thin enough, and not polished enough. I wanted to throw a Big Mac at him and swear but I just drunk dialed a few dozen times until I had properly embarrassed myself. I suppose he was not far off at the time. I was still reeling from my broken engagement and had no business dating at all.

I was about to take the paying gig at the comedy club when I got the call my dad was in the ER. I've never performed stand-up comedy again and

I'm ok with that. I did however; work in politics for a while. I was introduced as the "secret weapon" to political pundits, while working on a contentious congressional campaign. I was starting to think I was not supposed to be linked arm in arm *to* a man but instead, stand tall, self-assured and on my own, BEHIND ONE—perhaps next to a man, but I doubted I would ever be a part of one. I wish my dad had seen me in action on that campaign.

I suppose my soft spoken father was a little proud of me. After picking him up one day that summer before his death, he said to me,

"I never would have expected it from you, your success, the house, and the car, none of it." You're really something".

Flattered, stunned, and feeling as if I should tell him the truth about who I really was, I gave him all the cash that was in my wallet and dropped him at the house where he was staying.

He knew my house was soon to go into foreclosure and my beautiful white SUV with payments that were choking me now that I didn't make great money building other people's dreams, was soon to be returned . My elementary school secretary job would afford me a bit over unemployment but it was a start back to feeling useful again in a terrible economy after so many blows to the head. I was a long way from successful but I beamed pride to hear those words. It was a long overdue birthday gift, decades since the last time my dad remembered when my birthday even was.

Facebook entry: October 2, 2009

I sat down next to dad yesterday, snuggling up to him like a child. Unable to speak to anyone and looking as far away as his homeland of Ireland, Sissy said "Dad, Susie is sitting right next to you". Without missing a beat he looked down at me and said "Susie is like Spring"...and all is right in my heart. Xoxo. He died the next day.

Chapter Fourteen

Facebook entry: October 1, 2009

In brief moments of clarity I see the disgust in his eyes for what he has become. Not able to form a sentence, hold a pencil or share the fellowship that surrounds him is a bigger debt to pay than the cancer itself. To rob him of this life is tragic, to incarcerate his very soul thru which he now views the world trapped in a nightmare he can't wake up from is thievery.

In the end, I started to sleep by the couch, arranging the back couch pillows on the floor so I could be close to him if he needed me. Still not knowing the signs to look for, and light years away from my addiction to Google, I was winging it. After a few false alarms, I actually convinced myself that we were going to live this Utopian life where my dad needed me, my family was not the least bit dysfunctional and every day seemed like Easter Sunday.

I would light candles in the evening. The flames would dance off the metallic orange walls I painted in my living room. It felt like a sunset was gently closing out the day, all night long. It was these times I would sit and listen to his feverish escapades and talk him down from there or sometimes just act as if I was a part of the scene he was taking in. Not being someone that anyone in my family ever thought of as a leader or pillar of strength, I thought it was funny that I was guiding him into his next and final fantastical journey. I allowed him to describe people and places he was transporting to, and acknowledging this reality to allow him the escape from his true end which was clearer to him sometimes, than it was to me.

Dancing to Jim Croce in my kitchen with Rosalee, I felt as if I had harnessed all that was good in everyone, not realizing it would all return to normal after he left us.

I sat by his hospital bed in my living room on the last day. We watched the sun come up through the orange leaves on the large maple tree outside my front window. I emotionally melted down the day they brought the bed, 48 hours before he died. To me and to him, this was the end of the road. All the trays of lasagna, the bad puns, and the tall tales of the last few weeks were ending. He stopped being able to speak when the bed came. I'm not sure if he had really deteriorated that quickly or gave in. Just a week or so before, we gathered around him as I was sure by his restless night and slow breathing he was leaving us. His older sister (the plucky Irish woman who took no shit but loved so deeply), sat beside him urging him to "Go towards the light my brother, just go towards the light!"

Panicked, I reached for my Blackberry, to get the last picture of my dad before he left us. As the flash went off, my father, leapt to his feet. My aunt screamed, "Not that light. Sit down!!" This was the comic relief that we all needed and the jumpstart he needed to make it a several more precious days.

Sitting beside the hospital bed on that last day, I noticed he was damp. I changed his clothes, trying to gently remove his pants and shirt, his skin hurt him terribly. Being alive was as unpleasant as could be. He shivered as I pulled him to his feet, his arms draping over me, he was dead weight. I did this 3 times in two hours, from 6:00 am to 8:00 am. Tears rolled down my cheeks as I struggled to hold him up. I would not allow him a second where he felt like an object, but still human. With great care and gentleness, I would lay him back down each time, fix his pillow, and give him clean sheets and blankets. By the last time, my tears were hot, and my face flushed with anger. I was all alone. Not one sibling to help me and not even the caregiver to assist. It was me and him and he could not talk and I didn't know if he was in pain or even really conscious. Did he really know I was there? Did he care if he was in urine or had he checked out? I didn't know. I had no idea what death was supposed to be like except for movies and this was fast becoming a terrible one.

I hoisted him up on his feet to get the sweatpants all the way on and then to hold him up with one hand against my body as I flung the sheets off, trying desperately to throw a new one down. I had been telling him I loved him and I was so sorry he was in pain. So sorry I was moving him so slowly and so sorry this was happening at all. If life choices had not caged this free spirit, would it have changed this very moment? Would he have lived in a huge mansion in Scarsdale like his brother Jack had boasted time and time again because of his brilliance? Would he have been a happier person and would he have loved me the way I needed and deserved to be loved, if he had taken another path? Would my path have been different if I had not been rejected so long ago? Would I be chasing cars for so many years, until I stopped the chase all together?

Suddenly, as if he could feel my anguish, and as I looked up to apologize once again for keeping him upright, he looked directly into my eyes, with his, they were still so very blue and magnetic and he mouthed the words, "I love you".

My father died a few hours later. I had left the room to give my sisters time alone with him. I imagined they were experiencing their own pain left over from our complicated childhood.

When I heard the screams and walked into the living room, my sisters were both shrieking over and over, "What time is it?! Where is the clock?!" Apparently, marking his time of death was significant for them, for me, time was irrelevant. My youngest sat still holding his warm hand, I walked over towards him. I had left on the cassette player, some great Irish music and as I entered the room, I stood, soaking in the scene as if to capture it in my memory forever like a photograph, my own mind and demeanor was still, while my sisters started to wail and run for the clock. I peered out the front door, past the brilliant maple tree that was starting to show me what saying goodbye was really all about with its bright orange leaves. The mailman was leaving a final cassette in the mailbox from my uncle Jack, but it was too late. As I entered the room, I imagined I watched his last breath leave his body, but I realized, last breathe or not, he was gone for me, after our encounter just hours before. Nonetheless, I felt a wave of relief I'd never felt before—relief for him and my own true feelings to be named at a later date—relief after the last lasagna was consumed and the dishes were dried and put away.

My sister's actions were frantic and final, taking the pillow out from under his head and removing his partial. As if we needed to prepare him for a ceremonial funeral that would expire within the hour, I acquiesced and allowed them to be in charge for a few moments. My daughter looked up and asked, "What are they freaking out about?" and I had to break it to her that the hand she was holding was no longer connected to that spirit we all loved so much. She slowly slipped her hand from his and walked quietly into her room, so much to take in for a child of 12.

I called hospice and the funeral home. When they asked what time to come by, I told them 9:00 pm. I never really thought about the end. I only thought about each moment, maybe each hour but nothing further. I had wanted to soak in and savor every drop of my father's presence. I made a decision quickly and inspired by what I can't say, to give everyone a chance to say goodbye. With each phone call to the grandchildren, my brother, and my mom, I set up for one last gathering.

Chapter Fifteen

I waked my father in my living room for several hours. My sister planned and orchestrated his memorial a week later on my parents wedding anniversary. The grandchildren all got up, my daughter told a few bad jokes my dad would've loved and they sang his favorite song, "You are my Sunshine". I fell apart. He loved his children, especially when they were small and his grandchildren put a smile on his face. I suppose it was their childlike fascination with "The Artist" and the fact that he had not disappointed them the way he did us that made it natural for him to feel at ease with them. He didn't have to be responsible for them, he could just be himself.

One year later, I walked down the steps to the beach we had walked just a few years before, looking to sit as far from anyone I could in this public place. I gently poured his ashes on the beach in Sandsend, in the Scarborough district of North Yorkshire, England. The very same beach we walked a few years before, me following a few steps behind him, and the small child from town, holding his hand and hanging on his every word. At 38, I still knew my place. For my dad, this little boy was a wide eyed child who thought he was the world, unlike his daughter. Perhaps he'd seen me cry in the distance, in the glow of his taillights almost 30 years earlier….. or not. He certainly knew he played a huge role in my perception of love and my unquenchable need to be loved. That was obvious to anyone.

Sitting down on the wet sandy beach that stretched out for miles, I was reminded of my visit with him years earlier, when he turned half way back, still holding the child's hand and said, "If you started swimming, you'd eventually hit Norway", he turned back to the child and left me to ponder the information as he resumed his important conversation with the small boy. Sitting next to the ashes I had poured onto the sand, I watched the tide slowly come in and take them away. I traveled so far but once there, I didn't really want to leave them behind, as if the small bag I held, with my portion of my dad's remains was fairy dust. It was the first time I could say he was always with me but I knew in my head, he would always be with me whether I had something tangible to hold or not. I knew I had to return him to the sea and believe he would be with me regardless of physical bodies or parallel universes. A former diver and lobster fisherman, the lobster boat he kept docked in Rowayton, CT was named "The Skelligs" after the cliff he dived from in the 70's. "Skellig Michael" or "The Skelligs" is coincidentally where Luke Skywalker is discovered after years of solitude at the end of "The Force Awakens". I'd like to think his ashes went forward from Sandsend beach and took a hard right, moved down the English Channel, took another hard right, hit a pub in Cork and settled on Skelligs Michael for a bit. The sea was his home; or at least the happiest place he could be. I believe he loved his children but being a father was not for him at least not as gratifying as being a fisherman, an artist, a story teller or just being free.

As I sat filming the ocean creep in gracefully, almost respectful of my mission and the precious contents it carried out, ever so carefully, I was enraptured with the sounds of seagulls and children playing in the distance. For the first time I felt the finality of everything. My father's death, the men I loved who I should have known were never going to love me back, and the family who would never quite feel like family to me, no matter how hard I sought their approval and loyalty.

Closer and closer, it seemed, and with the same reverence my dad had for the sea, the sea obediently and quietly brought him home. To look for buried treasures as he had planned. Finding his fortune and never looking back.

I'd like to say there was a wonderful man who could understand my past, waiting for me at the end of all this to fill the holes left over by my father, but there wasn't, at least not yet. There is nothing magical about healing. It's a process and a journey. I've learned so much about me and as a mother who has made countless mistakes herself, my forgiveness is endless for both my parents. It is a constant awareness of my own strengths and flaws which actually pushes the childhood pain further from me. By growing in every way, I am able to see them as peers now. We are much more forgiving when our friends mess up but so much harder on our parents. The expectations for them to be smarter than us are unrealistic. Of course I am not the only person to have this revelation but I think it's so important to remember human kindness when we are counting the scars we have; kindness to ourselves and sometimes a pass to our parent. I'm an incredibly strong woman who overcame so much already. Perhaps I would not have the capacity to love if I had not been rejected. I practice extreme giving to those I find who don't have enough to eat. How would I empathize if I had not truly felt hunger and the shame that went with it? We can move past the intense pain of our childhood but certain scars will always remain. Scars, like tattoos tell a story of whom we are and where we've been. I wear them with honor now, because they don't define me, they just explain me, they remind me of my growth and they let me know with each scar formed, comes healing, they actually push me towards greatness I'm not afraid to pick an old scab and do the hard work to be whole.

I embrace this journey with my dad, the good, and the bad for it shaped me into who I am today, the good, and the bad. I accept all of me, and the place he had in my life to make me who I am and who I'm still becoming.
.

"The cure for pain is in the pain." - *Rumi*

The End.

Made in the USA
Columbia, SC
28 May 2018